LISA STERLING

In the
Palm
of His
Hands

Brilliant Books Literary
137 Forest Park Lane Thomasville
North Carolina 27360 USA

Because of the dynamic nature of the Internet, any web addresses or links contained in this book may have changed since publication and may no longer be valid. The views expressed in this work are solely those of the author and do not necessarily reflect the views of the publisher, and the publisher hereby disclaims any responsibility for them.

ISBN: 979-8-88945-181-5
eISBN: 979-8-88945-182-2

Printed in the United States of America

Day One

February 14th 2021

Philippians 3:12

Not that i have already obtained it or have already been made perfect, but I actively press on so that i may take hold of that for which Christ Jesus took hold of me and made me his own.

Perfection is a fickle word. On one hand we push ourselves to do right and work hard and learn from our mistakes. We try to teach our kids the same thing, hard work pays off and we will be rewarded. But what if that wasn't the case? What if instead of overachieving and pushing ourselves into exhaustion we take a step back and really see what all our hard work is getting us.

Is it pushing us toward God or pulling us away? Do we expect more from our kids than what we do from ourselves? Do our actions line up with our words? Do we put all our time and energy into everything else and put ourselves last on that list?

Philippians 3:17 Brothers and sisters, together follow my example and observe those who live by the pattern we gave you.

Who are we following? Or listening to? Ourselves, others or God? Just because we are made in God's image doesn't mean we act like him. Just because we speak doesn't mean it's the way we should be talking. If everything we have comes from God shouldn't we act like it? Instead of focusing on working hard each day we need to focus on working hard for God. He is our audience not people. He is who we should please and think of everytime we leave the house or interact with people. Because people see what's on the outside and God sees what's on the inside of us.

We live in an imperfect world and serve a perfect God. Does that mean we should be perfect in everything? Should we not do our best at everything? We will never attain perfection and should abandon that thought. But we can attain humbleness and be who God calls us to be. A better version of ourselves and not who we pretend to be.

my prayer..

Thank you Lord for today. For reminding me who you made me to be. For loving all of me including my mistakes. Help me to live like you today. In my words, actions and thoughts. And to put thoughts of perfection out of my head. Only you can do everything. amen.

Day Two

And the peace of God which transcends all understanding stands guard over your hearts and your minds in Christ Jesus.

When we look out our car window and its cold outside we don't see much. We have to turn the car on and then crank up the defrost to thaw out the windows. Our hearts are like that. IF we let bitterness,anger and resentment take up space in our hearts and minds we will succumb to those emotions and become embroiled in a game of what if's and should have's. But if we guard our hearts and minds and wrap ourselves in God's word and his prescence we will fold into him and not ourselves. Our peace doesn't come from ourselves our peace comes from the one who made us and knows what we are going through. Peace is like a spring it comes from knowing and trusting in the one who made us. Who knows us. And takes care of our every want and need.

my prayer..

Thank you Lord for providing for my need on a daily basis. I pray that you will guard my heart and mind against what the world is showing. Help me not to get sucked in but to stand firm and trust that you will do what you say you will do. In your name i pray amen.

Day Three

February 15, 2021

2 Corinthians 10:11

Let such people realize that what we say by word in letters when we are absent, is the same as what we are in action when present.

Our tongue is the only thing in our body that is hard to tame. It's the one thing that can lift someone up in one breath and then tear someone down in the next breath. It's been said that what we think and what we say are two different things. But in reality its the same thing only one comes out of our mouth and the other is in our head.

It takes more muscles to smile than to frown. It takes dedication and determination to stick with anything. Our words and actions are the same way. Our first inclination as human beings is to see the negative and speak the negative. It takes practice and work to be positive and to stay positive. I am sure there are some people who would disagree with me on that last statement. But if you really think about it there is some truth to that. Our human nature is prone to the opposite of what God wants for us. And if we really were to admit it to ourselves none of us have ever been or ever will be perfect.

In a good chunk of the new testament Paul states many times about attaining for perfection or striving towards perfection. Not once does he say we will be perfect. So if we want to be honest with ourselves, myself included, my words and my actions need to line up. Whether I am alone or with people it should always be the same. Wherever I am or whatever I am doing all of it should be to honor the one who made me. No matter what.

my prayer...

Lord, forgive me where I fail you. Show me those areas in my speech that I can improve. Show me how I can be more like you in every way, whether it be my thoughts, how I talk or how I treat those around me. In your name I pray, amen.

Day Four

February 23, 2021

Colossians 1:16

For by Him all things were created in heaven and earth, visible and invisible, whether thrones or dominions or rulers or authorities; all things were created and exist through Him and for him.

In school we studied history and learned about people, places and things that happened well before we were alive. We also studied science throughout school also. We learned how to study facts, make a hypothesis and test that theory to see if it holds water. Sometimes a microscope was needed to look at the smallest details and to look really close at the object.

What if we look at God that way? Do we see him as the Great I am or as someone who is far away and not interested in our lives? Is reading the bible just another book we read and then put it back on our shelf when we are done? If we were to be honest with ourselves we would realize that our life is not our own. Yes we own things on this planet but if today was your last day on earth can you take those things with you?

What is wrong with thinking that there is something greater than ourselves? That we aren't just put on this earth to exist? What's wrong with having faith and believing something that we can't always see that's in front of us? Are we too scared to look beyond ourselves and realize that our life is not our own?

Our choices don't define us. Our reaction and perception to the decisions in our life do define us. We can choose to believe or turn our back. Just like parenting we give our kids the facts to make good decisions whether or not they choose to follow is up to them. God does the same with us. He gives us the facts and whether we choose to follow him is up to us. What do you chose to believe?

my prayer for today…

Thank you for loving me. And thank you for not giving up on me. Help me to believe even when it's hard. Ground me in your word and help me to stand up for what I believe. In your name I pray, amen.

Day Five

Philippians 3:14

I press on toward the goal to win the prize of the upward call of God in Christ Jesus.

It's kind of funny how things are when we are kids. We work hard to achieve good grades to hopefully get into a college. Or in high school we work hard on that paper and research every detail put pen to paper and squeak by with a C even though we know we deserved at least a B. As adults we bust our humps every day at work in hopes of getting that promotion that is waiting. As stay at home parents being on call seven days a week a lot of what we do goes by unnoticed and there's not always a thank you involved.

What we consider success aren't always measured the same way that God measures success. Our way of thinking is not like God's way. What we strive to attain doesn't always bring us happiness and even that is short term. Our focus should be on listening to God's voice and following him. Because in the end the only thing that matters is what is waiting for us God's open arms and, "Well done my good and faithful servant."

my prayer..

I thank you Lord for who I am in you. That my successes aren't in what i do but what I do for you. Keep me strong and help me to keep my focus on you. Remind me every day who I can be and who I am in you. In your name i pray amen.

Day Six

John 15: 1,2

I am the true Vine, and my Father is the vinedresser.

Every branch in Me that does not bear fruit, He takes away; and every branch that continues to bear fruit, He prunes, so that it will bear more fruit.

Planting and maintaining a garden can be fun and lots of work. You find a spot, dig down to carefully place the seeds, water and then wait. At least that's what my kids thought when they were little. But in reality there is planning and prep work involved in having a garden. Finding just the right spot, measuring to make sure the area isn't too big or too small, researching what kind of garden you want to have, whether it be a flower or vegetable garden. There is lots of work that has to be done but in the end it's definitely worth it.

Our lives are very similiar. We need certain things to help us grow. Food, water, shelter, nurturing and supportive relationships. Just like that garden if you overwater it it will drown your garden and it won't be able to thrive. What has been planted will appear wilted or not look healthy. If there isn't enough sunlight to help the plants grow they will start looking stringy and growing out at different angles. Without sunlight it's growth will be stunted. If one doesn't tend to and take care of it at all it won't be a fruitful crop and just won't grow at all.

It's the same with being a christian or a new christian to be able to grow. In order to grow and become a seasoned Christian in our walk we need to do certain things that will help us grow and not hinder our own walk. Our nourishment or food comes from God's word, the bible. By reading it it feeds not only our minds but our heart. The sunlight we need to grow as a christian is spending time with other likeminded people. We need other people who will lift us up and help us along our way. To give us encouragement and love and sometimes not be afraid to tell us what we need to hear. Our pruning comes from God who starts to replace our old habits, old way of thinking and replace them with his ways, his thoughts. He challenges us to see him not just in the little things in our life but in everything. Eventually with just the right amount of sunlight, nourishment and encouragement we will start to see a new person evolving and our old ways die.. Our thoughts become his thoughts. Our new ways become his ways. And the things we thought were important and we put stock in aren't so important anymore.

my prayer for today..

Thank you Lord, for giving me what I need on a daily basis. Thank you for your love and encouragement each day. Remind me who I can be in you. Keep my feet planted firmly on the ground and not be distracted with everything that is going on around me. Give me the strength to face today and to do what you want me to do. In your name I pray amen.

Day Seven

Philippians 3:14

I press on toward the goal to win the prize of the upward call of God in Christ Jesus.

It's kind of funny how things are when we are kids. We work hard to achieve good grades to hopefully get into a college. Or in high school we work hard on that paper and research every detail put pen to paper and squeak by with a C even though we know we deserved at least a B. As adults we bust our humps every day at work in hopes of getting that promotion that is waiting. As stay at home parents being on call seven days a week a lot of what we do goes by unnoticed and there's not always a thank you involved.

What we consider success aren't always measured the same way that God measures success. Our way of thinking is not like God's way. What we strive to attain doesn't always bring us happiness and even that is short term. Our focus should be on listening to God's voice and following him. Because in the end the only thing that matters is what is waiting for us God's open arms and, "Well done my good and faithful servant."

my prayer..

I thank you Lord for who I am in you. That my successes aren't in what i do but what I do for you. Keep me strong and help me to keep my focus on you. Remind me every day who I can be and who I am in you. In your name i pray amen.

Day Eight

January 29th Friday

Ecclesiates 1:8,9

All things are wearisome;man is unable to speak.The eye is not satisfied by seeing or the ear filled with hearing.

What has been is what will be, and what has been done; there is nothing new under the sun.

Some might say today is the first day of the rest of your life.

I say each day could be your last and you never know when your last breath would be. With everything that is going on in the world today there are so many unknowns, uncertainties. Its so easy to fall into the fear trap.

What if i am late on my bills? How am I going to get everything done today? Why do my kids keep acting up and not listening to me? I just need five min to finish that report for my boss and make those follow up calls when will I find the time to do that? There is so much that needs to be done around here. There is just not enough time.

We get pulled into so many directions that our brains are left swirling and anxiety and frustration set in. Instead of fighting against everything that's pulling us in opposite directions step in. Instead of trying to figure out how to schedule and plan our day Be present in the moment. Take in the aroma of that first cup of coffee. Enjoy the moments when your teenager hugs you or thanks you for something you did. Revel in the fact you just celebrated your 25th wedding anniversary. The little things matter. And at the end of the day God sees the intention of our actions and our words not what we put on our daily " to do list."

So just like the capitol one commercial goes…

"Whats in your mind?"
"Whats taking up space in your heart?"
"Where do you store valuable treasures?"
"Whats important to you?"

My prayer for today:

Help me to remember whats really important. Remind me who I am in you and what I can do through with you. I know today there is so much that has my attention and I feel pulled in a million different directions. But even in this moment keep me grounded and help me to focus on what you have done for me and not what I need to do. Balance my thoughts and keep me centered so I can follow you throughout the day and not get swept up into my cloud of emotions. Show me how to be more like you and less like me. In your name i pray amen.

Day Nine

February 10, 2021

Psalm 34:4

I sought the Lord and He answered me, And delivered me from all my fears.

Fear comes in all sizes and shapes. It can hit at you from all angles and take you down like a tower of blocks. One minute we are fine and the next minute we take our eyes off the tower it comes tumbling down. Fear is just like that. When we aren't looking is when it hits. We let our guard down just for a moment and it can creep in and take us down. We can plan for the inevitable and be prepared and even still it will strike when we least expect it.

When our eyes are on God we are good. We don't have to worry about what comes next. It's when we take our eyes off him and focus on what's going on around us and our circumstance is when we get sucked in and start panicking. God hears and sees us. Because he loves us he doesn't let us go too far before he reels us back in. Even when we feel like we are at the end of our rope and can't figure out what to do we can trust that God has the details. Instead of focusing on what is happening and what could happen, focus instead on Who God is and trust he knows what he is doing. We aren't God and we can't do what he can. Because he loves us and knows what we need.

my prayer.

I thank you Father for your strength. For watching out for me even when I am not looking. Remind me Lord I cant do today without you. You are my rock, my foundation. You are what I need everyday. Please carry me as I go through my day and help me to focus on what you want for me and not what I want.

Day Ten

Psalm 141:3

Set a guard O Lord, over my mouth; Keep watch over the door of my lips.

Once upon a time we were all a child.. We thought like a child, talked like a child and acted like a child. We wanted things NOW! And sometimes we demanded our own way even when it wasn't for the best.I am sure there were times growing up we even threw a temper tantrum to get our way. If we are honest I think most kids are like that to some degree.

And then we grow up and become adults. In this day and age we have gotten so use to having things our way still. We still want things now and don't want to have to wait. Or we yell at the person who didn't use their blinker when they were turning. Sometimes it's easier to give advice then to take it and do what we are saying.

Our thoughts give way to how we act and how we speak. And if we aren't careful and thoughtful in how we present ourselves and how we say something it can be taken the wrong way. When God created us in his image he knew we would have struggles. Just like we teach our children when they are little think first then speak we need to follow that ourselves. God loves us for who we are not what we aren't or how we portray ourselves to others. How we treat and talk to others is how people will see us.

Lord, teach me today how to be more like you. Show me how to listen more and speak less. Remind me how I can be encouraging to those around me and help build others up instead of tearing them down with my words. In your name I pray amen.

Day Eleven

February 16, 2021

James 3:2

For we all stumble and sin in many ways. If anyone does not stumble in what he says, he is a perfect man, able to bridle his whole body and rein in his entire nature.

From the day we are born we are already dying. We live our lives in a sinful world and eventually we die in a sinful world. From the moment we come into this world our very nature is sinful. We are flawed.

As a newborn our very existence is put in the hands of the people who take care of us. Babies depend on the people that God puts in their lives. As a child we look up to those who we are around. If we see negative behaviors in the adults in our lives we will follow that example. But if we are lucky to be surrounded with love and good experiences we will show love because it has been taught.

And as a christian we start out as a newborn in Christ and we grow. Our experiences shape and mold us just like the people that God puts in our path. Some good, some bad. Our perspective can change and go in any direction at any time. Too many bad experiences can cloud our perspective and make one cautious and untrustful. But on the other side of the coin the more positive experiences we have our view will be different.

Just like a toddler beginning to walk, a newborn christian does the same thing. We have to walk before we run. Sometimes we will stumble and fall and other times we take off running and eventually we learn to fly gracefully or ungracefully. The christian life is not an easy one. There are many potholes along the way and challenges that will find us. But the thing to remember is that despite our sinful nature God is merciful and graceful. Because he loves us he knows what we can and can't handle.

my prayer for today…

Forgive me where I fail you Lord. Forgive my sinful human nature. I thank you for my life. Even though it hasn't been an easy. I know you have been with me every step of the way even when I feel uncertain or my emotions get in the way. Continue to remind me that you are still in charge because I can't do this on my own.

Day Twelve

October 28,2022

Sitting in a favorite place here in prospect. At the captain qurters grill right by the ohio river and 10 min from my apt. The phrase "I am centrally located." Comes to mind a lot. Because I am centrally located to everything. 5 min from the outdoor mall. 10 min from my new church. 10 from my new side nanny job. 30 min from my new full time job.

Moving to ky was the best idea that God could have given me. I keep saying I feel like abraham. When God told him this is where I want you and he moved to his new location he went without questioning. He trusted God andd God took care of him. Without fail, without any kind of conditions or parameters. God said, "Go." And Abraham did. He followed through and God not only provided but blessed him through that.

When God catches our attention and speaks to us our first inclination is," Me? Lord are you talking to me? Hang on I am on a phone call." or we respond with hesistation. Sometimes we tend to put off listening or dismissing God because we are too busy.

The almighty is never too busy for us. He is with us every day of the week not to mention by our side 365 days of the year. If he were to keep count on how many times we told him not right now or I am to busy we should be ashamed of ourselves. If he promises to take care of us and provide for our every need shouldnt that be enough to get our attention and focus more on him?

Day Thirteen

Haggai 1:5,6

Now therefore, thus says the Lord of hosts, "Consider your ways and thoughtfully reflect on your conduct!

You have planted much, but you harvest little; you eat, but you do not have enough; you drink, but you do not have enough to be intoxicated; you clothe yourselves, but no one is warm enough; and he who earns wages earns them just to put them in a bag with holes in it."

We are born, grow up, go to school and get an education. Graduate from h.s., and then either go to a trade school or college, get a job and work for the rest of our life. If we are lucky we meet someone who we want to spend the rest of our life with. Settle down, maybe have kids, take some vacations do some traveling and have a nice life.

Flash forward to the end of our life. What do we have to show for it? A nice house or apartment? Well behaved kids and a four legged friend who loves us unconditionally? A spouse who adores you?

We put money in our stocks and bonds so we can have a comfortable retirement. We have friends that we trust and share our secrets and can be vulnerable with.

Even with all that stuff that we have earned and worked so hard for our entire lives when we die we can't take it with us. It will still be here left behind. Waiting for someone else to go through and take of all the details.

As christians our stock and bonds are what we leave behind for those to remember us. How we treated those around us, or how we spoke to our family. We leave a piece of ourselves here on this earth to be remembered. What we do in the here and now, how we act in every situation and conduct ourselves that's what people will remember. Not the car that was driven, or the house that was left behind. But the life that you lived, And how you spoke and treated people. That is what will live on in the minds of those around you.

my prayer for today..

Help me Lord to be a reflection of you in my life every day. Let my words be few and my actions speak louder. Help me to look for your guidance and wisdom in every area of my life. Let me be the light to those around me so that when I am gone they will know you. In your name I pray, amen.

Day Fourteen

Psalm 118:22

The stone which the builders rejected
Has become the chief cornerstone.

When people think of February a few things come to mind: Abraham Lincon's Birthday, Black History and of course Valentine's day.

In today's culture, it's so much easier to drive through a fast food restaurant to save time versus going to the grocery store and grabbing what we need for a quick dinner. In our rush to get out there to work, we drop our keys and spend ten minutes scavenging for our keys which causes us to be late for work. Next, the realization hits us that our morning coffee that was poured into the travel mug is still sitting on the kitchen counter nicely waiting. So we make a detour for a cup of coffee to wake us up only to find ourselves inevitably waiting in the drive through line.

In our hurried up, always on the go world, everything runs on some kind of energy. From gas in our cars to food in our bodies, these things are done repetitively like we are on automatic pilot.

We tend to overlook and be forgetful about what we need for our survival, let alone our very soul. The God who loves us and created us in His image sits upon His throne waiting for us. He doesn't need sleep to be focused. And he doesn't need food to sustain himself and be nourished. he simply requires us to just be still and wait on him.

And the love we are seeking, the drive we need and the longing to fill us up comes from him. No amount of coffee will fill our soul soul up. But we can bank on God's word to fill us up and leave us hungering and waiting for more. And knowing we can lean on His waiting arms should drive us and know that he is waiting for us- because of His ultimate gift of love- Jesus.

Lisa Sterling
palm of his hand devotion

Day Fifteen

Philipians 4:6

Do not be anxious about anything, but in every situation, by prayer and petition, with thanksgiving, present your requests to God.

Anxiety is defined as an intense, excessive and persistent worry and fear about everyday situations. When God created man in his image he already knew we would struggle in this area.

He knows everything about us because he fashioned us. He knows us better than we know ourselves. In our minds we as human beings think we can tackle anything and when we fail we put pressure on ourselves because we failed to meet a certain expectation. In God's eye our failures tell our story.

No matter what our present situation is or how bad it looks it's not the end. Our minds make things look bigger than they really are and our emotions cloud the way we think and look. Even when our present situation looks bad God has this. He knows where you are and where you are going. He knows the outcome because he wrote our story. He knows what we can handle and when we reach our breaking point he is still there. Even when we can't see him or feel him. He is always there and has never left..

No matter what comes our way in life or how bad our circumstances are trusting and walking with God makes things easier and gives us that peace that only comes from him.

Heavenly Father, thank you for creating me and for today. No matter what comes my way I pray for the strength to handle and get through it with you. I can't do this on my own. Show me your grace and mercy and how I can show others who you are through my circumstance. In your name I pray, Amen.

Day Sixteen

Isaiah 43:2

When you pass through the waters, I will be with you; and when you pass through the rivers, they will not sweep over you. When you walk through the fire, you will not be burned; the flames will not set you ablaze.

Six months after my husband died I found myself spending a week in a psychiatric hospital. The only thing I was allowed to keep from my purse was my bible. Prior to being there I not only was dealing with a deep loss and heavy grief but other external stressors in my life. My world as I know it was scattered. My thoughts all over the place. My whole life and world had changed.

Grief is a funny word. Even though it's a five letter word it packs a big punch. Its like going through a boxing match and getting the snot kicked out of you. Everything you once believed in changes. The way you view yourself, your relationships with those around you changes. Life as you know it comes to a shrieking halt and everything stops. Even though the world is moving on you aren't.

I was drowning and I felt like I couldn't save myself. And it wasn't until I was in my room at the psychiatric hospital on the second night that I found myself reading the book of Isaiah and I came upon that chapter and that verse. Even though I felt like I was drowning in grief and wading through the mass of emotions I wasn't alone.

Even at my lowest point God never left me. He was there. He was present. And he was carrying me through to where I am today. And even though I couldn't see it then or see what he was doing I trusted him when I couldn't trust myself. I looked to him and he kept me from being swept away or burned. And he can do the same for you if you are open to him. Lean into him, cry out to him, scream whatever he can take it.

Thank you Father for who you are. For hearing me when I cry to you. Remind me I am not alone and you know what's best for me even when I don't understand. Thank you for all that you do for me. I love you.

Day Seventeen

2 Corinthinians 2:8

Wherefore I urge you to reaffirm your love for him.

When we say the words I love you whether it's to a spouse or our children or even our parents, does it just roll off our tongues without thinking or do we put thought and emotion behind it? Can our friends and family see Christ in us as we go through each day? It seems like when the holidays roll around we hear about peace on earth and goodwill to all men. And we also give of our time.

Why should it take the holidays to remind us what we should be doing 365 days a year? The birth of God's son Jesus, is a great reminder of how much we are loved. God sacrificed his own son who came to earth. He loves us that much that he was willing to sacrifice his own son for our many sins. What do we sacrifice on a daily basis? How do we show others around us that love?

It's very simple really. By putting others first and ourselves second. A simple word of encouragement, a phone call or even going and helping out a friend all show ways of being there. Just like Jesus example of how he shows his love to us we can do the same thing by being his hands and feet in a world that needs hope and love not condemnation and judgement.

Despite my many faults you love me Lord. No matter how foolish or ignorant I can be you still love me. Remind me today who you are and how I can be more like you not just in my actions but in how I speak. Amen.

Day Eighteen

Proverbs 30:31

Charm is deceitful and beauty is vain, but a woman who fears the Lord is to be praised.

I have always had a fascination and apprehension when it comes to snakes. From afar I think they are very beautiful and they move smoothly. But up close is totally different. If you are too close there is a good chance you could get bit. And then you have to outrun and get as far away from said snake.

Whereas if you were to look at one from behind a glass plate that's a different story. You would feel a little safer, maybe; not much but a little bit.

While charm and beauty go hand in hand that doesn't show what's on the inside. That snake like I was saying may look beautiful on the outside but on the inside it can be deadly and has the potential to either squeeze or bite you. As humans we have the capacity to show mercy, grace, love and patience. But if those qualities aren't honed and practiced then they are for nothing. If we say one thing but act another way then we are just like that snake. And our words and actions can leash out and attack those around us.

Beauty is not in the eye of the beholder. It's in how we talk, act and think. God wasn't messing around when he created us in his image. We have his qualities but that doesn't mean we always act or talk like him. There is only one that is perfect and it's not us. Beauty comes from within a humble heart

Thank you Lord for thinking of me when you created me. I thank you for your example that I have to follow. You know every part of me. Examine my heart and show me your truth so I can show those around me. Amen.

Day Nineteen

Proverbs 12:25

Anxiety in a man's heart weighs him down, but a good word makes him glad.

Anxiety is like an anvil. It's heavy and crushing. It chips away at you. It makes you question yourself and everyone around you. It starts to eat away at you and makes you feel like there's something wrong. It can lead to panic attacks, and if left unchecked and not dealt with can progress to medical problems among other things.

In this day and age there are so many reasons to feel anxiety and overwhelmed. With so many things going on in the world around us and in our own lives and in those around us it's easy to get caught up in the what if's and what not's. So here's what I am gonna say because I had to tell myself this..

STOP! BREATHE. Repeat.

No one said being alive or living on this earth would be easy. God never promised our lives would be carefree or that we wouldn't have problems, trials or even challenges every day. BUT, what he did promise is that with him and in him he would carry us through and give us the strength we need minute by minute. The trick is to remind ourselves that the only control we have is on what we say or what we do and how we react. Everything else is out of our control.

So the next time anxiety and panic are hammering away at you focus on him. Slow down your breathing. Close your eyes and just talk to Him. He is always there and sees all.

Even at my worst and darkest moments help me to reach out to you. Be my lifeline that i need. Guide my thoughts and calm my emotions. I give it all to you. Amen.

Closing Thoughts From The Author

I sincerely hope that you have enjoyed reading each day of this book and it has blessed you as much as it has me. I thoroughly enjoyed writing this.. It gave me a chance to put two of my favorite things together: reading God's word and writing. Throughout the book I have put snippets from different experiences in my life. I really feel like life is the best teacher. We can learn so much from our mistakes. And the beautiful thing is that no matter how often we fail it doesn't define who we are. We aren't defined by those things that have happened. In reality they are the things that make us who we are today. There are beauty in the ashes and hope for tomorrow.

I also want to thank those who have encouraged me and helped me along the way in my own journey. For being there for me when I needed it. For giving me that kick in the butt to move me along. And for always being honest with me even when I didn't want to hear it. Thank you to my parents for their love and support, my husband who loved me unconditionally no matter what and my biggest supporter. To my kids, who are now grown, and reminding me what matters most in life. And second to last my close group of friends who have shown me what it really means to be transparent and have helped keep me grounded even with all the craziness of my life. This is dedicated to Mike, Amy, Dan, William and Russ. I love you guys you are the best friends a girl could have. And most important above all else I thank you Lord for what you are doing in my life. Without you none of this would be possible.

Philippians 3:12

Not that I have already obtained this or am already perfect, but I press on to make it my own, because Christ has made me his own.

www.ingramcontent.com/pod-product-compliance
Lightning Source LLC
Chambersburg PA
CBHW020348130626
46549CB00003B/1358